THE BOUNCE

poems by

KARL MICHAEL IGLESIAS

Finishing Line Press
Georgetown, Kentucky

Y extendió Jehová su mano y tocó mi boca, y me dijo Jehová:
He aqui he puesto mis palabras en tu boca.
Mira que te he puesto en este día sobre naciones y sobre reinos,
para arrancar y destruir, para arruinar y derribar, para edificar y para
plantar.
—Jeremías 1: 9-10

You only good as what you come up against...
—Brad "Scarface" Jordan

THE BOUNCE

for Karla, Michelle
and all of the cousins

ACKNOWLEDGMENTS

The following publications have supported my work and have previously given earlier versions of these poems a home:

The Brooklyn Review, The Madison Review, The Westchester Review, Voicemail Poems, Lo-Fed Media, Sierra Nevada Review, Pigeon Pages NYC, Up The Staircase Quarterly, NO DEAR Magazine, and *Wisconsin Life.*

On Being Vulnerable was shortlisted for the 2022 Aesthetica Creative Writing Award.

This book was a finalist for the Robert Phillips Poetry Chapbook prize and was supported, in part, by the Kennedy Center's "Office Hours" Residency at the REACH.

Publisher: Leah Huete de Maines
Editor: Christen Kincaid
Cover Art: Karl Michael Iglesias
Author Photo: Dave Jeffers
Cover Design: Elizabeth Maines McCleavy

Order online: www.finishinglinepress.com
also available on amazon.com

Author inquiries and mail orders:
Finishing Line Press
PO Box 1626
Georgetown, Kentucky 40324
USA

Contents

THE UNUSUAL CIRCUMSTANCES OF A BIRTH 2

SWINGING 3

THE BOUNCE 4

FOR THE SCAR NEAR MY LEFT EYE WHICH MEANS
   THAT I HAVE COUSINS THAT LOVE ME 8

WARM 9

THROUGH HANDS 10

ON BEING VULNERABLE...11

WHEN YOU REALIZE WHO YOU'VE BECOME......................14

ACHILLES 16

SATELLITE 18

FORGIVENESS 20

THE ALTAR..22

SHELTER..23

I WAS PICKED UP FROM SCHOOL ON A HARLEY ONCE...24

HALF OF THE PARROTS RECOVERED.............................28

WE GROWN 29

PORTRAIT OF A BEACH I WANT TO WALK IN UNTIL
   I AM ALWAYS LOST..30

LOOKING BOTH WAYS...31

A NEW DANCE

THE UNUSUAL CIRCUMSTANCES OF A BIRTH

and when the baby arrives
still attached to a radial mother
both float mid-air
levitating from the gurney

a draping hospital gown
her saving limbs and long autumn hair
weighted toward the floor
heaven dangling her

by the bottom of her ribs   the nerve
and the room   full of rushed doctors
and nurses with country-wide eyes and facemasks
and open hands in latex gloves that prove

stringless and untouched
and how could this be possible
and one pair of latex hands receives
the newborn as they make their descent

from the suspended fortress
the doctor cuts the connection
between them   the mother
drops

SWINGING

my early skin stretched in the apartments off of third and mitchell.
a block away from the freeway. a sprint from the only basketball court
in the neighborhood and a parking lot, made mostly of grass,
that knew one day, it could be a park. a pink-sneeze every spring
and sour-red every summer. the apartments were surrounded by
our poppin' ass neighbors, *the crab apple trees*. would move a block
away to third and maple, to a house that was second from the corner.
and on the way home from allen-field elementary, which was on eighth
and lapham, after a long john and flamin' hot popcorn from the gas
station, my birthright was to climb up those trees. swing
from the wooden bars of an old shaky cage, it rained red and ripe.
snuck them home in the black plastic bag from the gas station, stuffed
in my backpack because mami thought it was nasty to eat off of some
southside neighborhood-tree. i'd wash the apples, of course, most of
the time. and during thursday night smackdown, i'd feast, and later
dreamt of being a park.

THE BOUNCE

Today I have awkwardly referred
to a new dance by the wrong name.

What was the dance?

It doesn't matter
how good I was
at staying the same boy
now I am tomorrow and the past—
washed even.
I accidentally
kill a teenager
leaving indoor track practice.

How do you always manage to be in such a rush?

The iced engine fan squeals impatient.
I am driving with my knees at first
down the side street of 19th
hands under my hamstrings
my breath is alive and my billowing passenger.
17 years old at the stop sign
turning onto Capitol.

Are you still there?

Snow, a quiet orange
from the street lights
my dying subaru impreza
turns mars rover

When was the last time you lost something?

and now felt like it was a good day
to prove I had the bounce
so I stepped on the gas

and the ashy snow sludges
back into the air
tires gripping blindly
into the intersection
and now the turn

How much do you think about yourself?

and now
the emergency
brake pulls
spinning
out of control
and I want to
stick the drift but
a fogged windshield
a spiral of tires
a new dance

on to a snow bank
sidewalk   someone's
front lawn.

Are you ashamed?

Nobody died
that day.

SOUTHSIDE FENCE

FOR THE SCAR NEAR MY LEFT EYE
WHICH MEANS THAT I HAVE COUSINS
THAT LOVE ME

which means we rug burn and remember the matches   which
means my cousin found his palms on my fall   which means we
went to church in spanish and spoke english   which means we
were bad as hell   which means we exercise   which means
I'd give my breath   which means we exhale with sudden hands
which means there was a neglected nail hanging out of a southside
fence   which means a little boy siren wails   which means
emergency   which means a little boy siren wails   which
means there was a neglected nail hanging out of a southside fence
which means we exhale with sudden hands   which means I'd
give my breath   which means we exercise   which means we
were bad as hell   which means we went to church in spanish and
spoke english   which means my cousin found his palms
on my fall   which means we rug burn and remember the
matches   which means that I have cousins that love me

WARM

I remember when one popped up on Easter weekend
family reunion. Where the primos stay home
as new parents, the titi's go to service
as daughters under their mother's roof

their father's roof. All the abuelos and
abuelitas have gone home   a long road trip
to a church convention in heaven. No one is sure
where all the tíos go.   Maybe it births at a warm

near your sternum and when you look down
you've discovered you've been baptized
with your niece's cheerio spit-up. There is a rag
for that and I don't change my sweater. It opens

with me being the uncle. With the yuca soaking
in morning water before being brought
to blade. Begins with patience. Before eventually
it goes down because in every long family,

there's a couple short tempers and I've been
an uncle since I was five. I know
where the hole in the hallway
comes from.

THROUGH HANDS

the first time you fell   in love
you were on the undercard

of a sold out Pay Per View
at Madison Square Garden

landing shots to the liver
jabbing jawbone   older men

cry in corners   their bass in
your chest   a brass instrument

you could kill someone in reach
you don't ever want to be

touched   puckered a leather fist
shuffle hip   you can barely stand

never been more wanted
press forward

huff   outstretched   you have nothing
left to hurt with

they will have to knock you out
cause' you been Puerto Rican   through

Cotto   Trinidad   Camacho   you
been bruising pride   trusting war

ON BEING VULNERABLE

the ocean invited me to twist
out the abandoned   a wrung out drop

you ever pour out a stream
of brew for someone
you have never met
because they remind you
of the homies?

i thought i would send what's left out
of my legs   to tread the murk and save
a body like my body   do you need
any help?   i can be vulnerable too and drown
in front of you
a buried bronze hand-sign
cut   from wrist
                        feel me?

(i thought i was shot
                        and you ran out of the parking lot
and i became concrete immortal   returning
for you)   out of time and into heavy tide

i draw in air
and my rib cage
fills with wrestlers
would you hold my body
down like your body?   hold your breath
like your brother?

LEMON TREE

WHEN YOU REALIZE WHO YOU'VE BECOME

you are on the verge
of arriving to the door.
There is someone
directly in front of you
and in front of them
and in front of them.
Behind you is a line too.
And someone who knows
you from Morse Middle School
And someone who knows you
from the church on 19th.
On the verge of a crossing rush
to enter the spot. I might dawn
a velvet rope and red footprints.
Stay on the inside of the loud
caution tape. I might pop
out my ID early and show
everyone around me. You see-
that's me, baby. Yes, I've been on
TV. Well, a TV was an idea
that didn't work out as intended.
And no, it didn't mean more
to my mom than not calling
last week. That's on me on the verge
of assumption. Me on the top
of the Maple street hill, fell
so many times, revolution
of story-scabs. Tumbling,
stay tumbling. Almost
to the front. I inspect
my identity closely.
Am I Puerto Rican
or just look like a lemon tree?
Infinite haircuts and I grow.
Pruned up. On the verge
of the bouncer. Who bounces
and isn't mean, just unforgiving.

On the verge of becoming
whoever I'll stumble out as.
The enlightened
scarecrow. Expiring.
Who was I before
I could spell
my name?
The bouncer,
grabs the ID and looks
at that man

then looks at me,

then looks at that man,

and looks at me.

ACHILLES

Pick up glass one shard at a time.
I can't believe my body
broke and again due to negligence. How much
is it worth?
I am aware
of the copay.

Bonding with stubborn fitness bands,
electronic stimulation coils
through pad and cable.
There is always pain
being attended to
a deep breath before I open
the door and I have to pay
for my session before hand
since I forgot twice already.

The junkyard starts
on the street and towers
behind barbed wire. There is what's left
of a wine hyundai elantra hatchback
a reflection of the one my mother drove. And I would
borrow after I reassured her
I wouldn't return totaled.
A tired muffler. Bearings
measured in miles.

Days of Our Lives is always on
after *New York Live*
but the assistants prefer the snap
of cricket. Groan of oak voices   whispering, *Jesus*
through a shoulder's contention.

When do we fully recover? A poster explains arthritis
and the coolant is leaking. I returned
in a boot I shed two weeks prior.

Cowering metal. The car rotting
into a parking spot and the glass has aged to jade.
Is there any pain   here?

The physical therapist has nothing
to say so we break
eye contact. And the two balance
bars ask, *What happened, you were doing
so good?* All the tires deflated.
And the stationary bike rolls
its eyes at the incline ramp
at my impatience.

The room is full of desperate
tendons. Tender parts still good.
Some glass breaks so
small it needs
to be swept.

SATELLITE

The day you leave
back to your plants and Indiana
I pick up where we left off
throwing away clothes
I didn't wear
and birthday cards
that didn't age well.
Letting go
of all my once-goods.

After the door closes
I remember.
I forgot my keys.
I forgot

what I always drum my pockets for
every time I'm between the threshold-
sitting on the glass table
near the couch.

I appreciate how when you're here,
there is someone inside
waiting or not but with the potential
to open up. Grateful for how my name echos
from down the hall. When you first arrived

I forgot to kiss you goodnight
and you invited me
to be grateful. Now I want to kiss everyone
good morning. Everyone, my brother.
My sister. Thank you, nourishment.

Standing outside Apartment 1
with my hand over my heart
grateful to have someone
inside to call out for.
To drum a window at 3 am
when I've lost my keys.

Thank you, listener.

Grateful for the church
in your phone.
Thank you, Sunday.
A woman is in love
hunched over a small screen
grateful to be present. Her service
streaming live.   *Gracias señor, gracias señor, gracias señor.*
Sobbing and must be grateful for
what I'm grateful for because

I am crying in the other room
at my own juncture with God. Our doors
open. Both of us who smack our lips
when we cry
annoyed with how long
how long it has taken us
to be grateful.

FORGIVENESS

i.

The best gift you can give
is a broken chain. All the guilty links resolved.
Take it off of you.
Take it off of me.

ii.

Don't be afraid
when there is no privacy with God
or with marriage. I am amazed
that my mom still asks about my father.

iii.

Let's say we are at church, it's ok, come as you are
I bring adolescence. A year of new self, a coming of age.
You, come as you are and we'll worry about the rest later.
This church has a live latin band, like the one outside of heaven's
barbed wire fence where you forgot your bag of debt, all the loans
you didn't pay. But just come anyway. A member of the youth group
is coming down the aisle in a dark hood and scythe
and in a roar of drums another young man two homecomings older
is in an all white robe carrying a sword of light. An angel
not a savior. Theater requires great seriousness. Anyway, the sky
opens where there was once a roof and the two are battling, striking
down the isles all for the souls of those who have sinned. Lightning
on top of a hill. Moving upstage. The pastor scorns,
This was forgiveness before the death of Jesus.

iv.

One time
I let
my daughter
I haven't
had yet
run into
the street
and all
I did
was yell
and hope
the road
didn't swallow
her. One
time you
will marry
me despite
all of
me. Two
grapes moshing
into wine.
I am
already sorry.

v.

Union of dueling swords.
Maybe true love is just who you've decided to forgive
for the rest of your life.

THE ALTAR

The Altar is a release of the shoulders. An apartment locking to keep
the light in. What lace cloth. What walk way. What veil. We light
the candles together like at a wedding and all our guests are dancing
and all our guests are settled spirits. Brass and wooden frames. A last
smile in a cold desert. Into soft dust a skeleton key turns.
All of our guests are a field of families we have gathered as flowers.
All of our guests are ghosts. A gathering of old frames
that rest cheek to cheek. If the dead can learn to live on, why can't
we? The altar is prime real estate. The rest happens here. As if
one day, we will join the quiet rest. The altar roars as audience.
As starving stomach. No one had to die for the altar but
the altar honors the dead. More people will die and the altar
will master the grief with candles. The altar is orange with
marigolds. The marigolds are orange like an altar on fire.
Mask over an aging face. How chill masks the desert.
The way the earth covers our body. The altar is
where we meet. Where your grandpa teaches you english
and mine talks God to me in Spanish. God invented the altar.
And the altar invented the flame
and the author and the morning.
And I've been thinking a lot about you
asking   *Why is everyone dying?*   I gave you a candle
and you gave me a black lighter. I should not have responded
with a quiet desert. Should not have retreated
into a frame, a fireplace. You heavy-sleep for two
more hours and you kissed me on the way back to the kitchen. Lit
a humble incense. The reason we all have to die is
to find a more accessible love.
Welcome, Welcome, Welcome. We met
at the altar, the distant faces in our faces.
A lasting field, coming to visit, to see us
together.

SHELTER

Do you remember
when you stepped on
the baby chick?

I wouldn't have known
but we heard the bones
surrender. Feathers
of yellow star dahlia
under the biggest boot
I knew. An accident
on your face. Is that
what happens to the fragile?
I do not know you
for your mistakes.

You gather what's left
of the baby bird. Place it under
a cup. And I can't remember
the exact words you conjured
but it must have been my name
and your name, forward and in reverse, pouring
from an hourglass. I wish I could fall
into your face. You gentle-drum on the table
to complete the ritual. I could play the rhythm
for you right now but I don't play
with magic. You lift the cup
and the chick whistles baby and hops alive.

How else was I supposed to look at you?

I WAS PICKED UP FROM SCHOOL ON A HARLEY ONCE

God called the light day, and the darkness He called night. Called me
into a room that was only dark from the outside. Called me
to the office to take my inhaler. God called off often. And sometimes
God called us outside for a word. God called him my father. I don't
really know where my father got his name from but
he gave it to an older brother like a bruise.

There he is. Light backpack. Little me, making his way down the
side of the school until- a bubbling wine-colored Harley Davidson
Sportster. I know how close you can get to an explosion. My black
bowl cut walks with Adamina, who God called my first girlfriend
in the second grade. Which meant she was a girl and my friend. I
remember being in love with how brave she was through her lisp and
gap teeth. I need an explanation for how I fit into the helmet. Was the
heavyweight championship belt a replica? She walked with me and
filled my backpack.

Well, who names you? Who was I before I was called, like a planet,
unobserved. God called me to orbit. Called me a car after closing time.
A rare flower that needs to have a way to be remembered. It started
with a wish. I wish I could go back to when I was a full mouth of sound
ready to avalanche, my primary mode of changing. Can you imagine
being named after a number? Named *Starless*? Or *Somber*?

I have a screaming eagle who looks like me. *Hey Champ*. God called
him *Father* and he calls me *Champ*. Adamina giggles, *Ha! Hey Champ!?*
She was quick to name me a joke. I remember being a little surprised
too. I had never been called that before by anyone. *Champ*. I never
won anything but my cousin wrestling matches on mattresses.

He balances me on the backseat and I squeeze him over thunder-glide.
Ascending on this floating island. A skipping rock
across block. Does anybody else see us possessed? For the first time?
Admiring burning steel. Is that love behind the noise? When will I

get my scent of leather? I will always remember this as the closest we've ever been to dying together. Caught in the exhaust. An

explosion passed on. We are a war reenactment, an independence

parade coming down *Historic Mitchell Street.* We are what is left.

The gust of confetti. How many possibilities have we exhausted?

How old until I am exhausted? No doubt. Vibrations rolling

through me as a hundred sneakers released to asphalt recess. Free /

shook. A bandanna is a flag over here. Rolling in black paisley.

Eastbound. Passing 9th Street. This was about having a name and

holding on.

WE GROWN

HALF OF THE PARROTS RECOVERED

the block is pecking through the early motions. showing up
was half of the struggle and the struggle was a beach
worth of sand. recovery is a spiritual process that could fill
a brooklyn tree with parrots; more of a ritual than a protest.
the parrots flew in on a journal entry and boy, are their wings
tired of thinking they can make a difference. the cafecito seems
to be part of this revolution too and the summer sidewalk has begun
to crawl. the trees we got last year have become neighbor-kin
and have dressed up in migrating quill. outside my window,
are thousands of childhood days that follow me in technicolor

plumage. they have filled the trees like sap, these days i collect,
and repeat as folklore. a branch is reaching out, to affirm the self—
and who am i to deny who i am? a branch is filled with
potential flight and a history of beaks that intend on
laying low until viejito. repeating name after name after name
after name after name after saying a prayer for a boy who died in
a protest in milwaukee for the right to righteousness. another says
a joke about imposter syndrome. one repeated it unknowing of its
place of origin. another repeated it and the truth made it burst-angels
like a pillow fight. one is repairing their spanish as they speak.

WE GROWN

and now he claws his way
out of the throat
he is the stuck lump
has the humble nerve to ask
where does the road go from here
from the open mouth of smoke
a type of magic I spell
like a given name

slipping between
the evenings of teeth
he stumbles from the blood tongue
in a wisconsin tank top
sand khaki shorts
he digs into a galaxy of lint
and on the lip
are a line of sudden graduates

flipping cups and trying to finish
he can't breathe and needs
the heaven-fields of mint
he wants to breakfast the fried
mornings over red plates again
leave you a message
written in a deck of cards
Wants to offer lake mendota

a plunge. A ghost in the eyes.
His face refusing to melt.
The color runs out
onto the summer dock, and leaps
and now he's here, with me
spending four days shaking
gripping me grief
as we groan.

PORTRAIT AS A BEACH I WANT TO WALK IN
UNTIL I AM ALWAYS LOST

> *"tomorrow I will add another word to my list*
> *maybe make it sweet"*
> —Cydney Edwards

tomorrow i hear the sudden hush of empty / tomorrow i digest
tomorrow over a steaming cup of tomorrow / i am not ready but
cannot wait for tomorrow / tomorrow been watching my moves
lately but don't watch me   watch tomorrow / i'll shower tomorrow /
tomorrow found me asleep in my long day / tomorrow picked me up
and washed my face in a fountain of may / i saw myself fresh greens
and clean / tomorrow i sun / tomorrow son's me all the time and i'm
used to that because tomorrow raised me / tomorrow raised me right
down the street from a melted winter / tomorrow brings lunch when
i'm not ready for any advice. tomorrow tatted on my face / walk new
york to the train / if tomorrow comes for me in the middle of the
night wake my sleepy ass up and pray for me / for tomorrow i might
make a light out of myself / tomorrow is long-will / morning eyes see
tomorrow / tomorrow i spring and spin marigolds / kiss after perreo/
i enter as passionate coal and invite a brass song / a fire lights my
feet / i part from dark / doubt all script and direction and tomorrow
swells / tomorrow i remind / call me tomorrow

LOOKING BOTH WAYS

I found the last corner store on the southside that wasn't a gas station
or a restaurant. I thought it closed down. At one point,
we knew to kiss our tíos and our titís and how much it meant to
them. Visiting your cousins was a brown bag bursting with dime-
prized sixlets, jaw breakers and mary janes. A fitted hat filled
with bright ideas we'd use on the nights the power went out.
A group of summer kids: the one who always had his shirt off,
his sister, the trio of brothers three years apart, my sister. All of us
found the corner store now and are running across greenfield ave to
the candy quick like someone was waiting to run us over like a sweet
sweep of gazelles where speed was a sword of a discovery.
Looking in both directions. At one point, they still allowed all of us
inside of the store at the same time and beer is in the back and candy
is behind glass and we are all pointing because tío
is cashing out and we all receive.

Except the youngest one, she is upset
she can't get the *extra* big candy bar
and would rather get nothing at all
like she knows what a pout is worth
and she won't budge and lower stock.
The sun at noon in July. Like titi Julie
is still alive. I am definitely not awake.   *Wait.*   Wait
for the total. I hurry behind the littlest one,
who is gazelle running into the street.
And there is no corner store.
Wait.   *One day*   *you'll only remember*   *the sweetness. Only*
the sweetness.   Of all your family-jokes   *on the inside*
        of every tin wrapper.   She enters the intersection
and is not looking anywhere but up.   *Wait. Wait,*   *remember.*
Remember what we practiced.

MORE GRATITUDE

Thank you God

for the support of the following institutions Hunts Point Alliance for Children, Urban Word NYC, New York Foundation for the Arts, Poetry Society of America, Brooklyn Poets, Adirondack Center for Writing, NYC Artist Corps, The Kennedy Center, The Public Theater, Hi-Arts NYC, The Office of Multicultural Arts Initiatives, University of Wisconsin, Rufus King International High School, Morse Middle School, Allen-Field Elementary.

for my SLB Brothers and First Wave family. A community I will forever need and love

for the words and support of Danez Smith, Ricardo Maldonado, and Sofia Snow

for the care and love given to my work by Ittai Wong, Will Giles, James Gavins and Yomalis Rosario

for the Kan Yama Kan community, the words of Hala Alyan

for the Emotional Historians community, especially the mentorship, wisdom, and friendship of Jon Sands

for the Supa Dupa Fresh community: Shout out to Rico Frederick, Jive Poetic, Mahogany L. Browne, and Adam Falkner

for Christen Kincaid and Finishing Line Press

for Genesis Selena Tornes

for all of my family. The rays that burst from my mother in every direction. As well as the new stars I fall into orbit with every day.

Rest in peace, Titi July, Israel and Nelida Laureano, Andrew Thomas, and Cydney Edwards- my sister and forever editor.

Originally from Milwaukee, WI, **Karl Michael Iglesias** is a Puerto Rican actor, director, and the author of *Catch a Glow*. His work can be read in the *Madison Review, Westchester Review, Sierra Nevada Review, Pigeon Pages NYC, Up The Staircase Quarterly, Breakwater Review, The Florida Review, RHINO Poetry, Kweli Journal, Haymarket Books' Breakbeat Poet Anthology, NO DEAR Magazine, Brooklyn Review,* and *The Academy of American Poets' Poem-a-Day*. Karl lives in Brooklyn, New York.

9 798888 387955